REFLECTIONS OF A NONAGENARIAN

Reflections of a Nonagenarian

by
Sydney M. Kleeman

Mountain State Press
Charleston, WV

Jacket Design: Sharon Harms
Image Associates

This is a Mountain State Press book produced in affiliation
with the University of Charleston. Mountain State Press is
solely responsible for editorial decisions.

Acknowledgments

I wish to acknowledge the wonderful assistance of my granddaughter Emily Kleeman who was so helpful in so many ways and even encouraged me to keep on writing my poems.

And to Beverly Calhoun, my good friend and administrative assistant, who enabled me to critique my own poems and assisted me tremendously in bringing about the publication of my first book.

I gratefully acknowledge Doctor Alfred Phister for his fine friendship and great professional care and interest--which have made our lives so much more livable, pleasurable and meaningful and enabled me to continue to write my poetry.

I wish to sincerely thank Dr. William C. Plumley whose professionalism and patience encouraged me to continue my poetic efforts and persuaded me to publish a slim volume of my poetry. His advice and counsel were most helpful and most welcome.

Thanks to Ina Taylor whose sincere interest, experience, and dedication to her helpful pursuit of gracious living for our family added so very much to my ability to cope with the problems in publishing my poems in my evening years.

Finally, I am most grateful to Cathy Pleska for her untiring diligence, interest, and ability in editing and bringing together all the diverse elements necessary to publish my poems. My sincere appreciation and thanks.

Reflections of a Nonagenarian

no•na•ge•nar•i•an (ˌnɒ-nE-jE-ˈner-□-En)   1: a person whose age is in the nineties 2: someone with good luck and good genes who has something to say   3: Sydney M. Kleeman of Charleston, W.Va.

Dedication

This book of poems is dedicated to my wife
Beatrice Loeb Kleeman
My roommate for nearly seventy years
My best friend and most severe critic
My research assistant, travel companion
A world-class listener to tall tales
A language interpreter, par excellence
The best helpmate one could ever ask for
in any one lifetime.

Table of Contents

Preface

Good luck and good genes are the epitome of hope and expectations.

Nonagenarians who have an opportunity to find a new way of living are indeed blessed—perhaps even more than they recognize—because they can try to envision what may be in store for them.

Laughing in your childhood, studying in your teens, and contemplating your future on arriving at your maturing years may appear to be normal for some people. But—challenging the status quo in your 70's, protesting the powerful in your 80's, and then writing prose and poetry in your 90's—these, maybe, appear a bit odd in our society.

The faceless thing we call society rarely chooses its members—whose numbers most often appear a sum of all those diverse people who inhabit our planet. Yet, so few individuals appear to believe they have something to say—or to say it at least to the few who can be persuaded just to listen.

Introduction

The purpose of this book is to dedicate my poetic efforts to members of my family whose interest in humanity might persuade them to read and, perhaps, to understand.

Likewise, hopes and expectations for this book are directed to all members of the human community who might drop a tear, raise an eyebrow, even permit a frown or some laughter after reading some of the poetry with which I have deliberately taken "Poetic License," and more than a little protest.

I must request, however, that my kind readers try to forgive me for my nonagenarian traits.

Perhaps they may even empathize with my efforts to explore, to excite, to explain my protests and my poetic efforts, all of which have tested my frailty and abilities and even my purpose and mission in publishing these pieces.

Finally, I have taken the opportunity to try to relate what being a "nonagenarian" is all about, from someone who was lucky enough to have a ringside seat.

These, then, are my thoughts . . . .

ঙ Thoughts ৎ
—At Ninety-Two

11/18/96

What does a nonagenarian think about?
If he really thinks at all —

Or, is just staying alive enough
to nurture a little of the soul, challenge the mind,

Alter desire, satisfy craving to
discover what is left—if any.

Discovery?

Childhood memories,

The Boy Scout era, the tender foot days,
the Little League Baseball,

The fleeting teenage years.

And now, arriving at the evening years,
these problems bring to question

The challenge of age
and its process.

Often never understood and disregarded
but, finally seeing the light, you wonder if

Tomorrow was an opportunity—
one that has come and gone?

1

ℬ The End of an Era ℭ

—Anticipating the End of a Millennium

1/14/97

But the end is rarely an end—

But so often signifies a new beginning,
a New Era, a new area to discover,

An enchanted, unmarked daunting journey—
new landscapes, alternate playing fields,

Even better times, and a new universe
to see—to hold—and behold

With all the excitement of exploring
the secrets of so many galaxies,

Recalling all those memories of growing up
and then—growing older—

With all its complex time,
the nonagenarian years,

Leaving behind all those troubled times,
memorable goals, but never forgetting to remember

The past, unforgettable—
those ocean crossings, the sounds and sights

Of those lush jungles, the spectacular peaks
of all those famous fabled mountains,

The multicolored foliage of the verdant valleys,
the photographic recall—

But, still retaining hope, and expectation
for all those who have the Zest

To see tomorrow's horizons, that new era—
for all those who can meet those inevitable changes

That life and living always bring.

℘ Need ℘

4/20/91

We have seen the atom split,
the molecule bombarded,
The genes invaded in many ways
Their cures and curses
But what we haven't learned is
the formula for existence—
How to live in peace with diversity.

If the great minds on this Planet
could agree to combine
their talents and inherited characteristics
to create a new gene that would
provide mankind
with peace of mind, an aversion to war
and a caring society—
would they receive a Nobel Prize
or a lunacy award?

4

৪০ She ৫৩

4/12/91

She is my chief cook and bottle washer
my cabin mate and most severe critic
My old companion for 69 years and my
astute opponent in debate
A Challenger Deluxe, a persuader above reproach
worldly, educated, sophisticated
So how could she ever forgive herself
for falling in love with me!

ଔ The Human Race ଔ

4/14/91

After so many millennia, man has learned
new tricks and horrors
about Savagery, Genocide, Brutality
and Torture
So why is our civilization so often
referred to as The Human Race
When there is so little, and so seldom
any Humanity involved?

ა The Infidels ᄋᲕ

4/24/91

Who are really the Infidels today?
The ones who believe in diversity,
in Pluralism,
or the persons who demand uniformity
or activism,
or the radical right or far left
who know no compromise?

ဆ Foolishness ૡ

5/8/91

When you hear your aged husband
talking to the Cardinals—
how silly can he be,
And when you catch him conversing
with the Blue Jays,
it's difficult to find any conclusions
other than to believe
that it's almost as hopeless as
one talking to himself.

℘ Name Calling ℘

4/30/91

If people in their seventies
are called Septuagenarians
and if people in their eighties
are named Octogenarians—
What should persons
in their nineties be called,
the Deity's favorite human,
or just plain lucky?

☙ The Aged and the Aging ❧

11/17/91

Old is when the sunset has faded,
        the flame dies and the fire is out,
When the wood is burnt,
Curiosity gone, and opportunity
        remote, even nonexistent—
And Hope, Faith, and Prayer cannot bring
        the body and mind together again.

When the curtain in life
        begins to fall and the shadows beckon
And the bones begin to creak, and
        the Spirit begins to moan.
When memory slips away and fails, and
        the footsteps slow down, falter, and are
unsure,
Then, then only do you stop aging
        and surely begin to grow old.

ଛ Roots ଓ

9/16/91

Who are we, and
     why are we here . . .?
Where did we come from and
     what do we stand for?—
All those enigmas are part
     of the past, present, future,
Together with all those players for better
     or worse,
Who survived the perils of time and events!

Are we a blend, a microcosm of all those
     knaves, villains, heroes, and do-gooders
Who lived their allotted time, without benefit
     of history books and often memories
But who formed our lives with their
     diverse genes and mores,
And made us what we could either like to be
     or, what we really are today.

ℰ Politics ℛ

3/10/91

If Politics is the Art of Compromise
and the Forked Tongue,
Why is it that so many Politicians
are so insensitive to arrogance and egotism
And rarely learn the lessons
documented so many times
that Power is a fleeting Phenomenon
that often runs out faster than time itself?

℘ The Wailing Wall ℘

2/17/91

Who likes to lose his wealth,
his worldly goods,
the Fruits of his labor and perhaps
his inheritance too,
to give up what his indulgences
and enjoyments dictate
Even when his lifetime follies
are only paper profits?

ᔥ Timing ᔥ

3/10/91

The Story of countless persons' lives
is one of Timing—
Too Early or Too Late, but rarely
on Time
Being Early brings guffaws and
so on
But just Being there, just arriving, is
Quite a feat for some persons.
Sometimes!

ഔ Our Divided Country ଔ

1/2/96

What is happening to the world's
greatest melting pot?—

The crucible of diversity dividing
those struggling for uniformity,

The have-nots who dream
about having something,

The haves whose appetites
never quite satisfy their hunger,

Those who live—to let live
and those who care too little

About living, and lives of others
the ones, who stand up against

Those vigilant fighters against violence,
the screaming crowd, others who just run
away,

Yet, others who abdicate their birthright and
some who challenge the fundamentalists

15

And, others, who take refuge in ancient
philosophies,
some believe that the family

Is the "root of our society,"
still others who care about moral values—

Those who would be color blind
and others, who delight to divide by color,

So, who will put this divided country
together once again— ?

ℬ Today's Savages ℭ

1/20/96

Where did all those savages come from,
the killing fields? or

From outer space, visitors from another galaxy,
or make-believers, dressed in modern clothes,

Or incarnations of a millennium's past knaves
or, perhaps, modern robber barons, disguised

To look like historic earthlings
with centuries of inherited characteristics,

Even emulating those look-alike humans
acting like jungle beasts, in disguise,

Or, perhaps, just a part of an unwelcome
hierarchy, bent upon power and position,

Practicing the ancient art of arrogance and egotism
on a playground of naked concrete acres,

Or could they be esoteric
green-eyed horned monsters

That outer space has sent to our planet
to bring fear, futility and destruction

To the very roots of our society,

Or are they really
just dressed as politicians, statesmen and voyagers

In dark suits, black glasses with closed minds,
waging conflict between uniformity and diversity,

Ignoring environmental needs, violence and drugs
and bring to question

If man will ever find his conscience
and allow it to overcome?

Are these what man has wrought for himself?

℘ Distance ℘

12/22/96

Minds are often as unfathomable
as the great oceans

Which stretch distance, time and calendars
often beyond any enchantment

But whose vast mysterious universe
of space, galaxies and creatures

Often indicate that distance can be
as short as crossing a continent

Or as long as just around the corner
which—also can make one feel a millennium away

Or it can provide an enrichment
of relationships that tie families together

Even suggesting the alluring prize of paradise valley
so uncommon, in bridging intervening space

But always connecting Genes and Chromosomes
challenging those chasms of diversity

In families, friends, and pretenders
which as often finds enchantment

Hope and high expectations—to bridge the gap
between the great distances

That may—sometimes bring families and friends
together.

ℰℴ Conscience ℭℛ

8/4/96

If conscience plays such an important
part in human affairs

If it may really be the
arbitrator of the moral law—for some

If it can be awakened—at times
to solve mankind's indiscretions

Then why can't its chameleon colors
for good not evil prevail and

Why hasn't that unseen, unidentified
feeling, expression, philosophy and mind-set

That small void, so very often
the innermost sensitive area

Of morality often being better identified
by science, medicine, philosophers

Clergy, politicians—who
found it so difficult to locate and manage

To repair, replace, amend or even restore
what man has searched his soul for a Millennium

But often failed to identify and understand its secrets
that man has kept, so often, for himself and

Why has history recorded its timeless calendar
of blood and tears, failures and success

Good and evil, his frailty and fatalities
his creditability and his well-being

Testing time, always—that never finds
to provide those existing questions

So often asked to solve man's
great enigma, still so mysterious to mankind

Asking sometimes why do some humans
have a conscience

While others often—appear to exist
without one?

ॐ Expectations ∞

10/31/96

Expectations are as diverse and boundless
as the seven seas—

And as varied as human effort, thought, and
hopes.

If you expect nothing—
then anything that you receive is a bonus;

If you anticipate just a little—
then any attention you receive will delight you;

And you are far ahead of the game.

Then, you can go about your daily chores
          as if tomorrow will never arrive.

so very own cs
Our ^ Hills

4/12/96
11/11/96

These rolling hills, weathered mounds of mother earth
spewing nature's forty shades of Irish Green,

The stubby formations of the low Pyrenees
emulating nature's own inevitable way

Of painting its own portraits,
man's inheritance of past millennia

Pondering about his own hills' immortality
while contemplating man's mortal years

Where man and beast still wrestle
with the spirit and the treasures of the universe—

Each with his own predatory problems and future
but surrounded with wild life and wild flowers

All competing for existence, in a world
that reveals its secrets so sparingly

Always trying to see the grass grow
and flowering blossoms unfold

23

But despite its panorama of unmatched elegance
that man is trying too hard to emulate

To resist the many warnings that time
has failed to impress

Because nature is beautiful, but fragile,
and it's man's eternal option to cherish—or destroy

Because his hills will stand forever.

‫ℬℴ‬ Whose World Is It? ‫ℭℛ‬

8/24/92
10/28/96

How often have we heard
anyone claim a solitary ownership of the world or its
      problems?

Some people don't care, but a few do
and seek solutions badly needed—

Of the concentration camps,
the stary-eyed and emaciated bodies,

The human wrecks with hunger written all over them,
or challenge man's inhuman behavior

And harsh, callow treatment of his fellow man
that rivals the violence of the jungle's predators,

The decaying standards of morality of our time
whose invasion of family life is almost to the point of
      destruction

With great evidence of widespread destruction of the
roots of our society—

Turning their heads away from the needy and underserved
      and the increasing gap between the rich and poor

All—of which brings to question—Whose world is it?

ஓ You and Your Mountains* ஓ

6/8/96

What a really great day to remember
any of life's great pleasures—

To discover nature's spectacular creations,
your very first view of a great mountain,

One of Mother Earth's majestic magical peaks
with a view of the ladder of footsteps

Up to the craggy heights, above the cumulus clouds
as if piercing the roof of the world,

Challenging the skills, experience, and discipline
of all those adventurous men who would conquer

Those wondrous mountains, their hazards and pitfalls
which withstood many millennia of nature's battles,

Its challenge of man's quest for fame
with its thunder, lightning and torrents,

Its raw atmosphere to discourage most humans
from ever seeing or ever understanding

Nature's own phenomenon in its own universe,
its primitive wild life, unmatched color of its wild flowers

And the roar of the predator, the cry of the hunted,
all of which is available, only to the favored few

Who have the appetite and the fortitude to take
that long journey to see it all.

*The Great Mountains—Fuji, Everest, Kilimanjaro, Jungfrau

ഏ On Borrowed Time ര

11/9/96

Is there really anyone who is
not living on borrowed time?

The calendar's race with
style and habit

We sometimes are placid, agreeable, kind and caring
often arrogant, egotistical,

Sometimes covering ourselves with glory,
sometimes shame,
causing wonder—

ଚ Out of Sight ଓ

8/30/96

Out of sight may be out of mind, but

The universe—the vastness of it,
producing distance, disillusion, disenchantment,

Upsetting relationships, blurring vision
disturbing the mind, engaging the psyche

Changing attitudes, perspectives,
often breaking ties, tearing the roots of families

Destroying the charm that distance brings,
contesting blood ties

And confounding consensus
from one generation to another.

๖ The Gap ಇ

2/5/96

The gap that disturbs, baffles, challenges
the very best of us—

Politicians, philosophers, clergy, the sages,
the newcomers to our daunting land,

The pervasive chasm which could destroy
everything that we hold dear,

The American Dream, its hopes and goals.

Widening the gap between the races, the rich, the
poor,
the challenging difference between the left and right.

Perhaps to narrow the widening gap,
addressing the gaps, the violence and drugs.

Even our democracy—
as we know it—could be destroyed.

℘ The Inhuman Race ℘

4/20/96

These people who
prefer war to peace, who are they? They

Thrive on violence, rape, suffering,
plunder and the killing fields,

Make a travesty of the Holocaust and
believe man's inhumanities are fiction,

Excel in arrogance, exceeded only
by egotism.

And where are the clergy, the politicians, the saviors
who could find a way to help in this dilemma?

Where is this greater force in the world
that reveals a higher authority that

Could warn man of his inhumanities—
why the silence?

❧ The Angry Old Man ❧

5/16/96

The anger came with
passion and fear

Uninvited, unwelcome,
a warning perhaps, of aging,

Bringing bewilderment, confusion, pain, anguish
and resentment—

I look around
and see what I thought I would never see,

Reckless uniformity,
a retreating to the jungle of terror and sameness,

Drugs, poverty and the widening gap.
So, what is left for an angry old man to do?

Just pray?—Or conjure up a storehouse of strength?

ೞ Horror Today ೞ

3/19/96

The unheeded cry of the tortured,
the forgotten ones behind barbed wire,

The century-old feuds, ethnic struggles
revived, once again, to test the human spirit,

Man's never-to-be-repeated Holocaust
once again, once more to disgrace,

To question, baffle, to stain
the way man behaves toward

His own flesh and blood, with
the world aghast, confused, bewildered—

Prisoners of their own bodies and minds
with no place to hide, no safe place to sleep,

No savior, or mentor, strong enough
to protect them, to stop the terror.

Will man ever learn his own historic lessons?—
and cry out, enough is enough!!

32

ℬ Borrowed Time ℭ

4/24/96

Does man ever perceive he may
be living on borrowed time—
loaned to use, or to squander?

The calendar's lessons are pristine, and
choice swings as wide as the horizon—
to stand against the madding crowd.

To challenge the status quo,
to fight for unpopular causes,
ignoring the ethnic cleansing, the killing fields—

Or, maybe the answer is to write a poem and
dream a little—
Maybe this is what borrowed time is for.

ඝ Call it—what you May ක

2/28/96

What would you call these lines—
prose, poetry, or

Just nonsense, akin to make-believe
so commonplace that you find it too dull

Even to allow it to enter your mind?—
so prosaic it always raises a doubt,

Perhaps happily adding a
a startling idea, stir your mind,

Invade you with a passionate
new sometimes strange emotion,

Altering judgment,
new dreams, even goals,

But sending you on a new mission, perhaps
to approve, improve, or disprove

Whatever you may wish to call it,
But it will never change what it really is.

ℰ Peace ℬ

8/16/93
1/24/96

Peace has been on a slippery slope
since the beginning of men.

Today, there is little peace,
only ticking time bombs—exploding,

Fragmenting man's delicate, fragile
calendar, between his moral indiscretions,

An interim of man's gasping for
his very breath of life

With fear, deception, hatred, cruelty and
mountain-high egos, uncaring

Bloodied by their own arrogance and conceit,
stoking the fires of hatred, for vanity and gain,

Bringing catastrophe, violence, the killing fields,
reversing peaceful pursuits for strife and conflict—

A no-man's-land, between madness and meanness,
a valley between the greening hills and

Drawing hope from all inevitable rights—
perhaps, an oasis for uncommon people.

℘ The Looking Glass ℘

"A parable for almost anyone"

3/8/95

Will your mirror tell it all,
who you are, what you wish to be, or

Even what you never were but thought you could be,
what you really didn't like to see—but did?

Did your mirror reflect your mind,
did it reveal all those wrinkles, pimples, dimples,

The gray hair, stooping shoulders,
your calm, quiet, peaceful mind?

Or maybe your temper, impatience, indecision—and
did your mirror tell it all, even what you didn't want to
   know?

Did it reproach, startle or challenge,
or did you see someone you never knew,

    Or even wanted to know?

℘ Laughter ℘

11/9/95

Laughter challenges those frozen faces,
the scowls and forehead wrinkles of gloom.

Laughter is the tonic of the ages,
perhaps inherited from the Greek Gods

Who knew that if man has not learned by now to laugh at
himself, why should he ever laugh at all?

ꕥ Chutzpah ꕥ

11/4/95

When is there enough Chutzpah?—
To really have your say,

To adopt reason instead of posturing, or
How much is enough?

To reform our environment, education, welfare,
challenge yesterday's lesson, tomorrow's realism,

To fight the mean, the ugly, the rogues in society
to stand up and be counted.

New
⁚ The ^ Banana Republic ⁜

12/20/95

This hemisphere is full of history—
knights' tales, conquest, corruption,

Killing Fields, Savagery and Power Players,
seeking riches, building towers of Babel.

The Incas, Aztecs, Spaniards and Portuguese.
All gave history its lessons

Of violence, slavery, power and politics,
establishing a widening gap between

The meek and the powerful, often
creating a chasm of darkness and indifference,

Establishing a Hierarchy of Elitism,
a pinnacle of power that brought

Fame, politics, a ruling scepter,
ignoring the social capital needed to

Combat social ills and needs,
disregarding human values and moral standards,

But, finally asking, is this the
new Banana Republic modern man has acquired

By his arrogance, elitism, and moral values
that history has long recorded, many times

But rarely learned, bringing him so bleak a future
as uncertain as yesterday?—

As questionable even as today
perhaps, with doubts for tomorrow.

"A fluid for all seasons"

9/12/95

Where do all the tears come from and

Who invented this arcane fluid?

Perhaps the God of Forgiveness, or the angel of
    remembrance

Who became disenchanted with

All the earth people—a millennium ago.

Or did the clouds in the heavens produce those fluids

Which so often bring out both the

Best and worst in all of us?

Sometimes—soothing the psyche and the soul,

Calming the spirit, challenging the peace of mind,

Even alleviating the pain of boredom and daily chores,

Often a paradox for the future,

But often assuaging life's anxieties,

41

But with all the frustration of love and hardship,

Even life and death.

Tears often come from those being savaged,

The victims of insensitivity

Which surely bathe life's struggles,

The handmaiden of both the past and the present—adversity
    and success

Sometimes—with such sweet parting and to remember

that on other occasions all the tomorrows may bring

More tears to soothe their feelings.

Often a mirror reflection of inner thoughts,

Tears are the fluid of all ages—all peoples—

Man's legacy.

℘ Bitter Sweet ℘

11/1/95

Who likes to see the days
  go so swiftly—

As the light disappears before
  its appointed time,

As day is subdued by darkness
   and the rain and stormy weather arrives,

The flowers wither, disappear,
  the trees shed their foliage.

Nature once again works
  its miracle of change,

Making colors only it could invent, for
  time never loiters, never stops

To announce the season's inevitable changes
  but, bitter sweet, or not

Just being alive is really enough.

ℰℴ Fear ℰℴ

3/28/95

The Heavens thundered, the clouds wept
the sky was covered with darkness,

Lit only by brilliant bolts of lightning,
bringing fear, consternation, and questions,

Perhaps a warning to listen once again
to the lessons learned, now long forgotten,

The litany of fears that bedeviled for centuries,
that rattled the bones, bringing tensions

That freeze the muscles, chatter the teeth,
slow the bloodstream, curtail circulation,

Challenge the psyche, mystify the mind,
frighten, terrorize, and freeze the instincts,

Destabilize the emotions—and fearing all this,
man must still meet his daily struggles

With his fear of diversity, and his refuge in uniformity.
Is it any wonder that all these anxieties

Have made for a fearful life?

44

🔊 The American Dream 🔉

11/9/95

Who were they, who dared to dream
    The American Dream?

Who challenged the barriers
to join the daunting melting pot of immigrants in the West?

Of strange, esoteric places, so far away,
a land of promise and enigmas.

Who were these peculiar-looking foreigners
from diverse areas of our world,

Born with a spirit, hope and desire,
with aspirations to challenge,

To escape the forgettable past of
fear, violence, poverty and persecution,

To find freedom, diversity and plenty?
Some endured.

But when did the dream begin to fade?

The memories of the past become a puzzle for the future,
a conflict between changing times and ideas?

The Dream, once a reality for so many
became possible only for a few,

Now, a Dream faded almost beyond recognition,
the spirit so universally bent,

It has nearly faded, but may come alive once again,
if the need for work itself survives.

ဢ The Madding Crowd ೞ

9/22/95

Who will stand up against the madding crowd,

Have his voice heard on high?

Stand alone, if necessary,

and protest the ever-present tide of public opinion,

When uniformity—not diversity—appears

To be the order of the day?

Who has the fortitude to be different

In a society that encourages conformity, and

Will dare to make decisions,

Challenge the extreme,

Protect the unprotected?

And who will question the "prevailing gospel," and

Not fear failure, disgrace or ostracism, yet

Who will risk reputation, position, even the future

To find new paths for a better tomorrow?

Who will have the patience of Job

And will stand up against the madding crowd?

      Any takers?

ℰ The Animal Society ℛ

4/21/95

What kind of world can this be
when men and animals are Wannabees,

When people act like animals would
and animals behave like persons should,

And demented, erotic persons go awry,
destroy life, limb, property, without even a cry,

Wantonly kill, without reason or excuse,
for pleasure and greed for no possible use,

People with appetites for power, position and riches,
leaving a trail of horror, against those they call bitches,

More holocaust without rhyme, reason or heed,
but never ashamed of their inhuman deeds?

Animals and humans trade places in life
that thwarts even the law of the jungle, so rife

That even history is bewildered at the blow
that caused civilization's latest show

That man has brought upon himself, blood on his hands
that no jungle law or human conscience can stand.

But who is to say when these inhumanities will end,
when man will listen before his spirit bends,

Before finding violence, savagery, rape and plunder
that shake the foundation of our world asunder?

And man, unwittingly destroying himself and his grace,
is caught up in his own frenetic pace,

So the inevitable fact that we face today
allows the jungle its inevitable way.

ඖ The Expendables ಞ

12/12/95

Who are those people, so very new to society?—
not the rich, the super rich,

The middle class, or the very poor,
the downsized, downgraded, down and out,

The new under class, the expendables
freed from work, against their own will

By the power structure of the powerful elite
in finance, government, industry, who believe

The end always justifies the means
replacing loyalty, hard work, empathy, fair play

With profit, greed, riches, bonus for a few,
destroying so many lives so quickly

Sacrificing health, security, family, life stability
without regard to today or to tomorrow's consequences—

The dehumanizing of our human values
creating a wider chasm between classes,

Bringing daunting social and economic change
to so many who are ill-prepared to combat the future.

The debate must begin—
Are all these humans really expendable?

51

꧁ The Day of Reckoning ꧂

10/12/95

The clouds wept, as if
nothing were left in the heavens.

And the sky became misty, cloudy, as if
to warn all those who should be wary

Of man's historic inhumanities,
never learning his own timeless lessons,

But pointing toward the day of reckoning
to those bewildered, questioning, apprehensive,

Seeking answers and solutions to their new dilemmas,
a test of faith, a time for revelations,

For retrospection, repentance, decisions for all
that was left undone, in those few allotted years.

How fast did all those decades go, too swiftly
and before your mind could even catch its breath

And all the years of opportunity, perhaps wasted,
but, still believing, that many new ones exist, even now

With hope, desire, faith and action for
all those who would help themselves.

Perhaps it may all take place
in another place, far away

Where deeds, not tears, will prevail,
where each one has his own special way,

His own full day.

‍ℬ Who Am I? ℭ

11/21/95

Have you ever asked yourself—
Who am I?

Am I just another human
with mere genes and molecules?

Why am I here, for what purpose,
if any—

To justify my own existence,
to prove I am my brother's keeper,

To challenge the status quo,
combat our daunting paradise,

Oppose vigorously what I perceive
is a "moral crisis,"

Provide a purpose, mission, or a goal
for myself, or even for others?

Or do I subscribe to pride and prejudice
and just mind my own affairs?

ဆ Old Bones ஜ

1/20/94

Time has its own incredible way
of making bones grow older,

Often wearing down the marrow
while permitting the limbs to become brittle

And creak, crack and cripple.

He might learn
before it's too old to matter!

℘ The Prisoner ℘

10/13/94

When the evening of your life
delivers you to new, arcane fields

And the appetite for new escapades,
new opportunities and experiences wanes,

Even appears to disappear from the horizon,
leaving you to your own devices—

And when your body doesn't respond to
what your mind commands and

You are left with feverish options
in meeting the dark shades of evening—

You ask, can you escape from yourself
even to see tomorrow's horizon?

ဢ Dreams ᥩ

7/3/94

Whoever invented dreams, where do they come from?—
the enigma of generations, seeking answers to timeless
     questions.

They arrive without notice, then fade into eternity,
rarely leaving a memory to cherish

And often not even a trace of the fantasies
are retrieved.

But, without dreams, the future may be
destitute, bleak and empty and

Without dreams—tomorrow may never be.

ℬ Peace, Again ℛ

12/14/94

Peace, that rich, rare, interim between
strife, contention and struggle.

Those quiet times of reflection
and thoughtful contemplation.

The temporary lull before the storming
of man's many temples.

Then finding human skull and rubble
in man's inhumanity to man.

Peace is the bright sunlight before
a world of hatred and darkness arises.

It is history's method of registering its own
account of behavior.

Those few gracious days man enjoys
before he falls from grace.

From the curse of another Holocaust and
its ethnic cleansing, savagery and barbaric actions.

So, before man returns to the law of the jungle
and the strangulation of his society, he may find peace.

But only if he recalls history's lessons
long forgotten, and never learned.

ઠ Poetry ଔ

The Other Definition

2/21/94

Poetry may be the meeting
    of mind and soul,

A venture in
    fantasy,

The past challenged,
    new hopes distilled.

Perhaps this, then, is poetry.

෨ Temper ଔ

"A new recitation of a very old trait"

1/29/94

Temper is the impulsive explosion—
of mind and matter,

A paradox, maybe, of psyche and
brash genes, and not a little of

Tantrums, passion and impatience—
mainly on others, espeically if not a little.

๛ Getting Well with a Little Help ๛

12/17/94
10/24/96

Healing requires some adversity,
coping with what was never anticipated,

What could never happen,
the unlikely, unknown tomorrows—

All unrehearsed, sometimes unwelcomed,
that herald the body's strength, resources, just

To persuade the future that it must,
With a little help from good luck and

A lot of help from good genes,
improve, especially with an extra helping of hope,
and maybe some charity.

"As I See It"

4/29/95

Some poems startle,
Some protest,
Some stir,
Some stimulate,
Some challenge,
Some disturb,
Some even caress;
Others prick,
Confront,
Gouge,
Punch,
And that, perhaps, is poetry, or this.

"A Mind-Set for All Ages"

5/12/93

This characteristic is not a modern-day invention:
   It's as old as the beginning of time,

As arcane as mystery,
      as fatuous as evil,

As disreputable as pretense,
      as promising as an excuse,

As evasive as truth—
      this thing called psychological deafness.

৪ Morning ৫

9/3/93

That rare time when

Eyes begin to open,

Ears start to listen,

Mind begins to search,

Psyche invites—

To locate the real self, the real purpose,

Then the day, once again, slips away

Before it hardly has begun,

And the search begins anew.

Oh, my—

໐ The Status Quo ໐

1/1/93

Is it fun or is it fantasy to believe
      that what has always been is always so,

Keeping a childlike faith that everything
      that was, still is?

Or is it both?

℘ Hope ℘

11/11/93

Hope is the stuff that dreams
        are made of:
The fuse that
        dispels despair,
The confidence that initiates
        challenge,
The inspiration that turns
        to illusion—
The antithesis of grief, depression,
        melancholy, and despondency.
Hope is learning to listen,
        civilization's ultimate necessity.

ಬಿ Evening ಲ

11/7/93

Evening brings its inevitable darkness:

What has long been forgotten returns,
unsteady, but still there,

Somewhat diminished,
somewhat real,

Sanguine and bittersweet,
pain and pleasure—

But I enjoy what remains of the evening glow,
For it is still there.

಄ Crisis Today ೞ

6/12/92

Time and the good earth
have been tenuous partners and

Long before the arrival of the first calendar,
men and women of diverse cultures,

Diverse of hope and expectation,

Apparently unstoppable,
a chorus to avoid Armageddon,

The killing fields, concentration camps,
disregarding history's lessons,

Bent upon power and position, questioning if
man is really a part of humanity,

But have time and the good earth
Been good lovers?

ଏ Spring ଓ

Where is spring, after such
    a winter nightmare?

So many people are seeking
    its forty shades of green.

With all of its tomorrows,
    can spring be far away?

ໝ Tomorrow ๛

"For the Aging and the Aged"

8/19/92

Prepared or not, tomorrow will arrive
      as surely as there was yesterday—
With sweet expectations, hopeful serenity and
      predictable human frailty:
Power, position, and undue ambition will struggle
      with hope,
In the ageless conflict,
        for tomorrow's opportunity of being better
        than yesterday's or today's.

ℬ The Foolish and the Fooled ℭ

8/28/92

The game of make-believe is
     as old as human conniving,

As disingenuous, as unpalatable as the
     Devil's advocate, his goals and objectives,

As short-lived as man's allotted earthly span,
     and despite history's repeated lessons

Often listened to, but seldom heard—
     man prefers the silly senseless posture
          of a fool's paradise.

ℰᴏ Name-Calling ℭᴙ

1/30/92

Name-calling
      has been a favorite pastime—
Hurling sticks and stones in disingenuous ways,
      hurting, bruising, wounding
With ugly fabrication,
      a luxurious labyrinth,
Sometimes tenuous.

Who, then, will be the first to throw stones, and
      who will pretend to have the license?

Kings and queens and the elite
      often indulged in their high privilege,
A pastime producing no winners,
      except, maybe, some name-calling.

℘ OverAge ℭ

1/3/92

Septuagenarian or Octogenarian is just
    a matter of degree

Of age, of aging, that should cover all
    the elements of a Final Enjoyable Spree,

Providing, of course, that the body and mind
    are in concert with a sublime rhyme

And the expectations don't overtax
    Time!

℘ Arrogance ℘

8/10/92

This age of arrogance reflects the
      consummate ego and the defiance of man:
A marriage of selfishness and self-serving,
      ignorance and moral cowardice,

Undue pride and insolence,
      haughtiness and imperviousness,
False superiority and superstition,
      immodesty and inferiority.

And their source?—
      the Gods of the Sea,
The steaming jungles, the frigid mountains?
      Or were they spawned by superstitious holy men?

℘ Evening Shadows ℘

7/20/92

The years disappear like water in the Sahara Sun,
      the calendar grudgingly gives up its dates,
The young become elders
      often before their goals are achieved,

The lucky ones become octogenarians
      with varied expectations and hopeful
      security, and
Life's span appears too short at best
      while events often overtake time before life
      is done.

Then time passes more swiftly than the flight of light
      and disappears into the fragile tomorrows,
while shadows inevitably lengthen into a
      specter of what could have been.

๛ Blame ๏

4/6/92

Blame appears almost everywhere—
      more than enough for everyone:
It's in the air, the ozone, the atmosphere,
      permeating the Halls of Congress,
The sovereign territories of old and emerging nations,
      the Halls of Academia, the Police Academy,
          the Courts,
The Clergy, the Domain of Workers, Healers,
      the Greedy, the Shakers and the Movers.

The politicians blame taxpayers,
      taxpayers blame their Legislature,
The jailers blame the inmates,
      the criminals blame society,
Labor blames capitalism,
      the clergy indict their parishioners,
The parishioners blame the Deity,
      and so it goes, in this blaming age!

But Don't blame me if these three little words
      become our new National Anthem.
I only set it in words,
      not in stone.

ᔍ Craven Idols ᔎ

2/8/92

A millennium ago man's habits, ideas,
        philosophy, objectives and lifestyles
appeared to be esoteric, curious,
        even fatuous, rarely idealistic.
His gods of thunder and lightning,
        of flora and fauna, the sun and the moon,
were just some among many he invented
        with his dreams and mythology, to
                guide his life.

The Greeks, Romans, Assyrians, the builders
        of Babel,
unleashed their talent and imagination
        to create and worship their craven idols.
Sponsored by their high priests,
        often with fear, but with respect for
                the unknown,
but also inspired by gold and silver,
        and chattels, intrigue,
and self-fulfilling laws they influenced.

And how have all the history books, the empirical
        records, recorded this?
Have we summed it up as
        false icons of a millennium's age,
Made by men
        with feet of clay?

ᔄ The Last Hurrah ᖇ

For all their sadness, joy and Reservations
—Hurrahs—
Are events to be remembered in
Every Era of Man's Existence
Because it often signals the Course of History,
changes Boundaries, uproots governments,
And sometimes even alters the very roots
of life itself.

Hurrahs are often said to be for the
young to bellow
From the bleachers and the grandstands:
they spew their wonderment,
Producing strange noise,
more than enough
to wake the neighborhoods, even some
cemeteries.

Yet, many Last Hurrahs will never be heard,
but this one has, if you can read.

∞ For Ever ∞

4/10/92

History records again and again man's arrogance,
     ego, and conceit in building
An empire, a civilization, a philosophy
     that he perceives will last forever:

The Assyrians, Babylonians, the Egyptians,
     the Romans and the Greeks,
The Mayans and the Aztecs,
     Mussolini and Hitler,

The tyrannical kings and queens and
     the men on horseback,
Communism, totalitarianism, authoritarianism.

But what has endured?
     An inconsistent past!

ಋ Modesty ಞ

4/14/92

Has modesty gone out of style, or
       was it really ever in vogue?—
The kings and queens, the Emperors and Presidents,
       the Dictators and Tyrants

All knew about it, but didn't practice it often.
       The Bible, religious chronicles, history books,
Family albums, encyclopedias, all have
       documented an awareness of it.

Where do we find
       the humble, demure, self-effacing?
Where can we learn about the elusive,
       in the Convents, Monasteries, Houses of Worship?

No college or university demands modesty
       as the price of entrance or degrees.
No job application says it's necessary
       to secure employment.

No marriage counselor includes this trait
       in advice to clients.
Surely no hierarchy in government or business
       appears to give it due credence.

So, what is all the fuss about?

And since human nature changes little
       even in the best or worst of times,
Modesty may never be in style!

℘ Violence and Vengeance ℧

—Then and Now

4/17/92

This place is not China
       and its brutal Tiananmen Square.
Nor is it Kurdistan
       with Iraqis slaughtering "unequals."
It is not India with its ethnic killings
       between Sikhs and Hindus.
It couldn't be Burma with their gross
       inhumanities to their own kind.
It isn't even this century's most notorious
       Genocide—The Holocaust,
Where six million humans failed to survive
       and cruel and despotic men stained
the name of humans forever,
       where history registered its indelible mark
Of torture, fear, persecution
       and human indignity
And senseless death and suffering abounded
       But—
              But—
What about our place, our planet—
       Now?
Have we learned
       anything from the awful past?
Did we remember, recant, reform
       our ways—or—

Did our society still allow guns to kill
        indiscriminately without reason or restraint
Where crime still overloads
        our jails and prisons?
Did we permit our "love canals" to
        defy health and environmental standards?
Didn't we identify or recognize the characteristics
        of dioxins and cancerous compounds
that were destroying our children and others?
            Did we turn our head
From the greenhouse gases and carbon dioxides,
        or did we just pretend
And look aside at the eternal conflict
        between economics and the environment
And allow our air, water and good earth
        to be polluted in order to save jobs
But bringing instead sickness, havoc and even death?
            Did we ignore
the ozone, its global warming and warning
        and continue to ignore and laugh at
The dire lessons it brought?
            Did we face the
        scientific facts of life—
Of underfunding AIDS, the scourge of
        this twentieth century?
How could we justify our record
        infant mortality—the highest of
any industrial nation on our planet?
                Why do our political bosses
Permit this senseless neglect of our people,
        even allow drugs to continue to
                maim, kill and destroy
Today's and even future generations,
            Why—Why—

82

Do we permit all this existing
            posturing and pandering
                    So—
                        So—
                                Today?
The name, the places, the circumstances
            the excuses and reasons—
All are changed for today's updated scenario
            but, we must remember,
                    that this place,
                            our place
            not then, but now—
Has its own killing field,
            just a different kind—
That goes on and on, infinitum,
            in this twentieth century
                    and nothing
has really changed from then to now—
                    except—
The time, place, methods and the actors.

℘ Narcissism ℘

7/13/91

Millions of people have fallen in love
       and history and literature have
Recorded these great and
       memorable love affairs and stories:
The psychologists and psychiatrists have
       given their blessing,
And even most churches have approved
       their divine right.

So what could be the problem
       with falling in love
When it has been so universally acclaimed
       throughout this planet's existence?
Could it be the foolish people who
       fall in love with themselves
And who surely deserve the very best
       from their misplaced narcissism?

Falling in love is far easier than
       it could ever have been believed
With your mother, father, sister or brother
       or even a cousin or two,
Or, perhaps with just a face, a stranger,
       or even with love itself.
So perhaps one of the greatest delusions of our time
       is falling in love with yourself.

ஐ Man's Future ☜

5/1/91

What is it that usurps man's mind,
      body and soul,
that produces the arrogance of power,
      conceit, egotism, and so often corrupts?
Is it raw power, status, gold or
      silver, chattels, or women,
or is it man's own stupidity, of never
      learning history's often repeated lessons?

The future is a part of yesterday, and
      even of today, but surely tomorrow
history's errors, record of failure and despair,
      today's dreams, curiosity, and opportunity—
So why does man have to prove, once again,
      he may be his own worst enemy,
by discarding his past and becoming the
      most endangered species alive today?

❧ Optimism ☙

10/12/91

Optimism is the breath of life that starts
       the flow of blood, of hope for better times,

Which often fuels inspiration, imagination,
       vigor, and discipline to pursue opportunity.

It stimulates the juices of curiosity and the
       appetite for excitement;

It formulates faith, brings on reality
       to achieve missions, attain goals, and

Sometimes success, even beyond dreams!

ᔕ Human Dilemma ᔓ

4/14/91

All the King's Statesmen and all
the Queen's Philosophers
And many Educators, Soothsayers
and Politicians
Have grappled with man's
aberrations for a millennium,
so why is our legacy today one of
sterility of thought, a vacuum of indifference,
an uncertain future?

ഔ An Apology ര

4/24/91

Who ever heard of apologizing for
being *numero uno?*
But we can't deny being number one
in Teenage Pregnancy, Murders by Teens,
and Number One also in percentage of our population
behind Prison Walls
And *Numero Uno* in Emission of Pollutants,
so does anyone have the colossal nerve
to disclaim having that questionable moniker
Number One?

Getting Married

"A narrative to learn from;
—an experience to live by"

7/5/92

Getting married is an age-old custom, but
staying married is almost a miracle;

Tying the Gordian Knot has become
Arcane and
losers rarely notice history

Winners—learn what relationships mean:

That eternal struggle between two humans
is as universal as life itself—

The Bees, Bats, Birds and the Beasts—
they have all done it and know how . . .

ༀ Getting Along ༀ

"A narrative about man's past and future"

5/19/97

Getting along is a problem as old
as time–

The eternal struggle
for territory, position, power,

Aligned with uncertainty and
animus toward fellow humans,

From his monstrous concrete palaces
his modern bumps, hurdles and circumstances,

The riots and burning cities
their violence and hazards,

The enigma of race—war and peace,
the inescapable heritage of that,

And, today—the demand
for uniformity

Instead of the commonality
          that bonds us in our love and suffering.

৪০ Conclusion ৩

It may take the patience of Job and all the king's horses and all the king's men—plus his sages—to help me put a lifetime of learning, thought, and experience into just one book of poems and meditations.

But perhaps there are still those who have a zest for living and the excitement for an unyielding chase who will share my "Poetic License," and then perhaps they, too, may be able to find their incentive to publish their own ideas--to spark a new agenda, to find a new path of opportunity or even a new venue and earn a chance to retrieve life's coveted Brass Ring as their reward.